Eliz[illegible]d
Jacob[illegible]hire

by

JANE STERLING

DALESMAN BOOKS
1973

20p

The Dalesman Publishing Company Limited
Clapham (via Lancaster)
Yorkshire

First published 1973

ISBN: 0 85206 197 8

Hortus Printing Co. Ltd., Burnley, Lancs.

CHAPTER I

Elizabethan Lancashire

THE first Elizabethan Age, from 1558 to 1603, was one of the greatest in English history. It was a time of increased prosperity, of new inventions, of voyages of discovery, the age of William Shakespeare, and the era which saw the defeat of the Spanish Armada and the establishment of Britain as a great sea power.

The end of the reign of Bloody Mary was welcomed by many people, including her half-sister, Elizabeth, who succeeded her. Elizabeth, the daughter of Henry VIII and his second wife Anne Boleyn, had been brought up as a Protestant. But she made it clear at the beginning of her reign that there were to be no fanatical reprisals for the persecution of the Protestants which had overshadowed her sister's reign. She had no wish to antagonise the Roman Catholics, but on the other hand she did not want to show favouritism to those Protestants, the Puritans, who wanted to see the Church reformed more drastically, doing away with all the ritual associated with Roman Catholicism. Many of the Puritans who had lived in exile during the reign of Mary, had been influenced by the ideas of Calvin, the Swiss reformer, and had returned to Elizabethan England burning with zeal for drastic reform in the Church.

The Elizabethan Church Settlement was an attempt at a compromise between such men and those who wished the Church of England to be "Catholic but without Pope". In the new Prayer Book of 1559 the wording used in the most important service, the Holy Communion, was a masterpiece of diplomacy, which could be accepted by those who retained the Catholic belief of the Real Presence of Christ at the Sacrament implied in the words "The body of Our Lord Jesus Christ which was given for thee, preserve thy body and soul unto everlasting life", whilst the Puritans who held the limited belief in the Spiritual Presence only, could accept the following sentence, "Take this and feed on Him in thy heart by faith with thanksgiving".

Three Lancashire men were prominent among those who helped the queen to define the doctrines of the English Church in 1662. All three, Alexander Nowell of Middleton, Edwin Sandys of Hawkshead, and Thomas Lever, had been exiles in Switzerland and all had Puritan views, though their enthusiasm for the ideas of Calvin varied in intensity. Both Edwin Sandys and Thomas Lever were strongly opposed to the ceremonies of the Catholic Church and were in favour of doing away with what they considered to be the superstitious trappings of religion – such things as the wearing of vestments by the clergy, the use of the sign of the cross at baptism and even the use of the ring in the marriage ceremony. Alexander Nowell, the Dean of St. Paul's, was chosen as the spokesman of the queen's advisers. He was a man greatly respected by religious thinkers of the time (in spite of the fact that he had once been rebuked by Queen Elizabeth when he was in the middle of delivering a sermon from the pulpit of St. Paul's). Nowell was in favour of compromise between the two opposing views and it was largely because of his influence that the settlement was so widely acceptable and has in fact remained the basis of the doctrine of the Church of England to the present day.

The new religious settlement was enforced by the new Act of Uniformity but Elizabeth was no religious fanatic and at least in the early years of her reign there was no persecution. Attendance at the parish church was compulsory – any who did not attend had to pay a fine of one shilling – but there was no law against the gentry worshipping in their own private chapels, and many of them were quite willing to pay the fines while continuing to worship in accordance with the rites of the Roman Catholic Church. Most of them would put in an appearance at the parish church from time to time and many even took Communion there as well as hearing the Catholic Mass in their own chapels.

Most of the landowning families of Lancashire were Roman Catholics and nearly all had their own private chapels, many of them with a resident priest (sometimes introduced into the household as a private tutor to the children). The laws about church attendance were particularly badly kept in Lancashire as many of the J.P.s, who had the job of enforcing the rules, were sympathetic towards the Roman Catholics or were unwilling to take action against their neighbours.

Later in her reign, however, it became impossible for Elizabeth to retain this "easy going" attitude to the Roman Catholics among her subjects. Severe measures were necessary in 1569 when many Roman Catholics took part in "The Rising of the North" – a rebellion intended to dethrone

Elizabeth and replace her with the Catholic Mary Queen of Scots who, while Elizabeth remained childless, was the next in line for the throne of England. Though the actual rising took place only in the north of England, the ringleaders had plotted for a general rising against Elizabeth, and one of the Lancashire gentlemen implicated in the plot was Sir John Southworth of Samlesbury Hall near Preston, who had been at Bath when there was "a great flocking of gentlemen upon pretence of taking the waters". The visit to the famous spa, where since Roman times the waters had been taken for all manner of rheumatic complaints, was only an excuse, for Bath was a place where meetings could be arranged and secret plots worked out without arousing suspicion.

The scheme for simultaneous risings in the north and south failed. Government spies revealed the plot and Sir John was taken to the house of the Bishop of London where efforts were made to convert him to the Anglican Church. Strangely enough, when Sir John refused, saying that he would always be faithful to the religion of his fathers, he was allowed to go back to Lancashire! John Southworth was fortunate, but his luck was not shared by the many northerners who took part in the rebellion – about 800 people were put to death for joining in this attempt to restore a Roman Catholic monarchy to England.

The Pope, Pius V, had given his support to the Rising of the North in 1569, and when it failed he drew up the famous Papal Bull against Elizabeth which was published in 1570. By this Bull the Pope decreed that all Roman Catholics in England were freed from "all manner of duty, fidelity and obedience to Elizabeth, pretended Queen of England" who, "because she oppressed the Roman Catholics, re-established the wicked ministers and preachers of impiety, abolished the sacrifice of Mass and all Catholic ceremonies", and had "a heart so obstinate and obdurate", was to receive the sentence of "Anathema" or excommunication from the Church.

Elizabeth's attitude to this Bull was that the Pope had no authority over her as head of the Church of England, and the main result of it was the intensifying of the laws against the Roman Catholics who had now received Papal authority for treasonable acts against their queen. Fines for non-attendance at the parish church were increased from 1s. to £5. It was decreed that Papal Bulls had no authority within the realm of England and that anyone making known the wishes of the Pope would be regarded as a traitor and die a traitor's death.

But there were many whose traditional allegiance to the Roman Catholic Church could not be broken. Though the training of priests in this country was impossible, many of the Lancashire gentry found ways to send their sons abroad to be trained and ordained and later to return in secret to their old homes or neighbourhood and minister to the faithful. One of the foremost Roman Catholic families in the county were the Allens whose home, Rossall Hall, stood on the Lancashire coast where Rossall School is now. The best known of the Allens is William Allen who became a cardinal of the Roman Catholic Church. William had been imprisoned in 1551 during the reign of the Protestant Edward VI but had risen to an important position during the reign of Mary. When the tables were turned again and Mary was succeeded by the Protestant Elizabeth, William Allen left the country and lived in exile in Europe. As he was well known to be one who was dedicated to the re-establishment of Roman Catholicism in England, Elizabeth's spies kept him under constant watch. When he secretly returned to his old home on the bleak coast of the Fylde, the sheriff of Lancashire was ordered to arrest Allen and others, "late ministers in the church who were justly deprived of their office for their contempt and obstinancy and who are yet or lately have been secretly maintained in private places in that our county of Lancaster". Mains Hall at Singleton, near Blackpool, is one of the places where Allen is traditionally believed to have been hidden while the sheriff's scouts searched in vain for him.

In 1568 Allen had founded the famous Roman Catholic college at Douai in Flanders, and it was from here that a few years later a steady stream of newly trained Roman Catholic priests began to return to England, "some in apparel as soldiers, mariners, merchants or gentlemen". There were always those who felt strongly enough about their religion to return to their homeland in an attempt to win her back to what they believed to be the true way, in spite of the fact that if they were caught celebrating Mass they were liable to the death penalty. They knew that they would always be able to find faithful Catholics who would shelter them, even though heavy penalties were inflicted on anyone giving help or shelter to a priest of Rome. After 1585 this was an offence which could be punished with death – one man was in fact put to death for giving a priest a pot of ale.

In the first part of Elizabeth's reign the main fear had been that the Roman Catholics would raise a rebellion to put Mary, Queen of Scots, on the throne of England. This had been the object of the Rising of the North and of numerous other plots. William Allen had been in constant contact with Mary and her execution in 1587 was a grievious blow to their hopes. The hopes of those Roman Catholics who wished to see Elizabeth dethroned were transferred to King Philip of Spain, the arch-enemy of Elizabeth, who in 1588 launched the great Armada against England hoping to destroy the power of the Elizabethan seamen and to restore the Roman Catholic faith to the kingdom of the heretical Elizabeth.

Many Roman Catholics in England had been ready to welcome Mary Queen of Scots as their lawful queen in place of Elizabeth, but to the majority of them it was another matter when it came to supporting the claims of a foreign king. It says much for their national feeling that most of the Catholics in England remained true to Elizabeth rather than face foreign domination by the King of Spain, Roman Catholic though he was.

There were others, however, who were working to remove Elizabeth and to restore Roman Catholicism to England, whatever the cost, and among these was the exiled Lancastrian, William Allen. While Philip II was preparing his great Armada, the Pope instructed Allen to write "The Admonition to the Nobility and People of England" in which he tried to rally the English to support Philip against Elizabeth. Philip himself regarded Allen as one of Elizabeth's most dangerous enemies and it was on Philip's particular recommendation that the Pope rewarded Allen's services to the Roman Catholic cause by making him a cardinal. The King of Spain wrote of Cardinal Allen, "He has morals, learning, judgement, great acquaintance with everything in the Kingdom (England) and with the negotiations for its conversion and the instruments of all these have been and are his disciples, of whom so many have suffered martyrdom. The purple of his (Cardinal's) hat may be said to be dyed in the blood of martyrs whom he has educated".

Because Cardinal Allen was a Lancashire man and had been brought up on the coast, and as it was known that Philip II and his advisers had been in close touch with him, it was at first thought possible that Philip was planning to invade England by making a landing somewhere along the coast of Lancashire. In 1585 the old Norman castle at Lancaster, by then practically in ruins, had been rebuilt and strengthened. You can still see on the north wall of the keep an inscription which reads, "When Elizabeth was Queen, and Richard Assheton was sheriff, in the year 1585, this tower was restored".

The Peel of Fouldrey where Lambert Simnel had landed in an abortive attempt to dethrone the first Tudor was considered to be a likely place for a landing base in an all-out effort to oust the last of the Tudors. This is part of a letter the sheriff received warning him of the possibility: "Between Mylforde Haven in Wales and Carlisle on the borders of Scotland there is not one good haven for great shyppes to Lande or Ryde in, but one which is in the furthest part of Lancashire called the Pylle of ffloder. This same pylle is an old decayed Castell, sityated on the sea cost . . . What the Spanyerde meanes to do the Lorde knows, but all that country beinge knowen unto Doctor Allen yt is not unlyke but his direction will be used for some landynge ther".

The fortification of the Lancashire coast was unnecessary. When the Armada sailed it made for the south coast of England and in the English Channel the death blow was struck at the pride of Spain. The most that the people of Lancashire saw of the great Armada was when one ship of the battered remnant of the Spanish fleet tried to get back home by sailing round the Orkneys. It eventually drifted round the north-west coast of Lancashire and was dashed to pieces off the coast of Walney Island opposite the Peel of Fouldrey, where it had once been feared the mighty forces of Spain would land to crush the power of Elizabeth.

The defeat of the Armada ended the hopes of the restoration of Roman Catholicism as the recognised religion in England. Cardinal Allen, who had hoped to return to his native land as Archbishop of Canterbury, had to remain in exile for the rest of his life.

But the Roman Catholic religion still flourished in the land, and particularly in Lancashire. Even those Roman Catholics who had remained loyal to Elizabeth when she was threatened with destruction by Philip of Spain were not willing to accept her religious settlement and give up their old religion. In spite of persecution and heavy fines they continued to celebrate Mass and to give cover to the many priests who had returned from Cardinal Allen's college at Douai and to members of the Society of Jesus, an order formed with the object of restoring Roman Catholicism as the universal religion of Europe. Foremost of the Jesuits, as they are usually called, was Edmund Campion who himself visited Lancashire and is known to have been the guest of the Southworths at Samlesbury Hall and of their near neighbours, the Hoghtons of Hoghton Tower.

Elizabeth and her advisers were not blind to the need to keep a strict watch on certain Lancashire families and her chief minister, Lord Burghley, had a map drawn in 1590 showing the main houses in Lancashire and those which sheltered known recusants (those who would not attend the services of the Anglican Church). The map is an extremely

Borwick Hall, near Carnforth, an Elizabethan mansion incorporating a medieval pele tower.

interesting one as we have only one earlier map of the county, Saxton's map of 1577. Burghley's map makes no attempt at geographical accuracy, but it is a valuable record of the religious strife in the county in Elizabethan times.

One of the most fascinating features of many of the old houses of Lancashire is the large number of priest's holes and secret rooms that can still be seen in them. It was during the time of religious persecution in the Elizabethan period that most of these were built as hide-aways for priests for whom Elizabeth's spies and agents were continually searching.

Many houses were also extended or rebuilt during the Elizabethan period which saw increased prosperity throughout the land. The Tudor Age was one of settled government which put an end to civil strife of the Wars of the Roses. The careful economic policy of Henry VII, the first of the Tudor kings, had led to increased trade and to more settled domestic life than had been possible during the turbulent times of the late Middle Ages. One of the results was the building of new and much grander houses. In the Middle Ages, manor houses had been built as places of refuge – often they were surrounded by moats and had similar defences to castles. During Tudor times the houses developed into a home – much more money was spent on making it a pleasant and comfortable place for a family to live in, rather than a fortress which might have to be defended at any time against warring neighbours.

All over Elizabethan England, houses in the new style with large glass windows were built or old medieval manor houses given a new look by the addition of wings to give the familiar "E" or "H" shape of Elizabethan houses. In these new mansions the hall was still the most important room and the only one which was more than one storey high. Other rooms were added on each side, usually the servants' quarters on one side and the family apartments on the other.

This era of new building, or altering of existing buildings, was a great help to those who had something – or someone – to hide, and fortunately for them the new styles of building provided the opportunity for incorporating secret rooms which were very hard to detect. The "hides" are nearly always found in the family wing of the house, where priests could be kept out of sight of any gossiping servants.

One of the status symbols in the new Elizabethan houses was a chimney. During the Middle Ages smoke had (sometimes) escaped through a hole in the roof. The Elizabethans built elaborate fireplaces, often very ornately carved or decorated. From these smoke escaped through enormous chimneys of which the owners were so proud that often the long rows of tall chimney pots were decorated with spirals and carvings of all descriptions. But the wide chimney breast often had another use in Roman Catholic homes for it was possible to make a shelf high enough for a priest to hide in when the searchers came, and also possible to build an escape route for him to make a getaway when the coast was clear. The vicinity of the fireplace was often also used for an underfloor hide. Among the stone flags which covered the hearth there would be one loose stone which could be moved to reveal a hole large enough for a priest to hide in until the danger of discovery had passed.

Many of these holes have been discovered when new floors have been put in old houses.

During the Middle Ages it was fashionable to have tapestries on the walls. Made of loosely woven material embroidered with pictures or patterns in wool, they were also known as Arras hangings, the name referring to a town in northern France famous for their production. The use of these as wall-coverings survived in many places well into Tudor and later times. Father Arrowsmith, a Roman Catholic priest who was martyred early in the seventeenth century, said he remembered that when he was a child in Elizabethan Lancashire searchers came to ransack his father's house at Haydock, near Wigan, in search of priests. To make sure that no-one was concealed in the beds behind the tapestries they "stabbed with their swords the mattresses and Arras hangings of the rooms".

In many of the new Elizabethan houses, oak panelling was used instead of tapestries as a covering for the plastered walls. The panelling was made by first setting up a framework of narrow pieces of wood and then setting loose panels of oak behind them. It was fashionable to have doors panelled in the same way, so that the walls of a room presented one long panelled surface. Many of these long walls contained secret panels which were only known to the family and which could be opened to reveal yet another type of priest's hole. Often cupboards with panelled fronts, set into a wall, had a second door at the back which gave access to an escape passage. Hides and escape routes like this can be seen at Speke Hall near Liverpool and many other Elizabethan mansions which were owned by prominent Roman Catholics.

The ingenuity of the "hide maker" seems to have been unlimited. The vogue for wooden staircases to replace the old stone spiral type universal in the Middle Ages was utilised to great advantage. At Towneley Hall in Burnley there is a large hide about 16ft. square and 6ft. high. The room is made in the space between a lowered ceiling in one room and the floor of the gallery above. It was reached by moving one of the steps in the staircase and replacing it when the forbidden "massing priest" had concealed himself behind it. This particular hide is larger than most and is lined, like many others, with a mixture of clay and rushes so that the priest could move about without being heard.

Some hides are so small that it seems impossible that anyone could have hidden in them and remained alive, but great care was always taken to see that there was a good draught of air which eliminated the possibility of the secreted priest dying

Speke Hall, the Elizabethan home of the Norris family, is now owned by Liverpool Corporation.

of suffocation. An interesting example of a very tiny hide is at Chingle Hall, Goosnargh, where behind panelling there is a hide just big enough for a man to stand upright, but it would appear impossible for anyone to live with the panel in place. The hide-maker, however, had seen to it that air was available through an inlet in the outside wall.

Some of the houses which belonged to Roman Catholic families in Lancashire contained only small holes for concealing priests in the hope that they could be kept hidden while the searchers ransacked the house with the object of bringing another of the Popish priests to "justice". Other houses, which were important centres for receiving priests who came from abroad to start their mission in Lancashire, had much more elaborate systems. Speke Hall was one of these centres – priests arrived in ships which sailed up the Mersey and were concealed at Speke Hall until arrangements could be made for them to travel on to houses where they would be sympathetically received and supported. Edward Norris, who inherited Speke Hall in 1568, had extensive additions made to it in 1598. The Hall already contained secret rooms, including an eavesdropper's hole – an opening in the eaves over the entrance from which all visitors could be seen and heard. The eavesdropper could give warning to any in the house who did not wish their presence to be revealed. When Edward Norris added the new wing he took advantage of the new building as a cover for making a network of secret hides which were connected by secret passages to escape routes. During the last years of the reign of Elizabeth, countless priests must have used the hides at Speke Hall when they came to this country inspired by a passionate zeal for ministering to the Roman Catholic population of Lancashire.

In spite of the elaborate precautions taken to keep priests hidden from government spies, many of them were caught, tortured and put to death. During the last fifteen years of the reign of Queen Elizabeth about 250 people – nearly all Roman Catholic priests – were executed for adhering to the old religion. A large proportion of these were either Lancashire men or had connections with the county. There are some horrifying accounts of the sufferings of Roman Catholic martyrs during this period of persecution. Many of those who had celebrated mass and minstered to their people in Lancashire were caught by the priest hunters and cast into jails often in terrible conditions. In rat-infested prison cells they were questioned to make them reveal the names of families to whom they had administered the sacrements and if they refused to tell they were tortured – sometimes on the rack – in the hope that in extreme pain they would be willing to give away their secrets. One priest, after having needles pushed under his nails and being stretched on the rack until the torturer could boast that he was an inch longer than God had made him, was cast into a prison cell "where, not able to move hand or foot or any part of his body he lay in his clothes for 15 days together without bedding and in great pain and anguish". Father Gerard, a Roman Catholic priest and son of the owner of Bryn Hall near Wigan, describes his torture in his book *The Autobiography of an Elizabethan.*

In spite of the pain and anguish which they suffered, most of the priests refused to give the information the government wanted and eventually most of them suffered death on the charge of having been made a priest by Roman authority since the accession of the queen. An Act of Parliament of 1585 had made it a capital offence for any such priest to be in England. The condemned priests were dragged to the scaffold on wooden hurdles with their feet tied and their heads bumping on the muddy and rough roads. When the poor victim arrived

Elizabethan architecture. OPPOSITE PAGE:- TOP: *Rufford Old Hall, in which Shakespeare may have acted before he became famous as a playwright.* BOTTOM: *Hurstwood Hall, near Burnley, a manor house which has recently been restored.* THIS PAGE:- *The house at Hurstwood where the poet Edmund Spencer spent part of his youth.*

at the gallows he was expected to make a speech to the spectators with what little breath he had left after his exhausting "ride". The sentence was that he should be hanged, drawn and quartered, and as the condemned man was making his last speech he would be able to see close at hand the cauldron of pitch in which his head and quarters would be dipped when the executioner had done his gruesome job. Hanging in those days was a lengthy job as the use of a short rope resulted in death by slow strangulation. Whilst the prisoner was still struggling his body was cut down and chopped in pieces, the head and quarters usually being displayed in some prominent place as a grisly warning to those who felt inclined to disobey the laws of Elizabethan England.

Lancashire has certainly many connections with the darker side of Elizabethan life but in this it is exceptional as a county which predominantly cleaved to the Roman Catholic religion. The story of Elizabethan Lancashire also has its associations with the brighter side of the era. There is a possibility that the greatest of all Elizabethan writers, William Shakespeare himself, may have come to Lancashire as a member of a company of strolling players which visited Rufford Old Hall, the home of the Hesketh family, and Knowsley Hall, the seat of the great Stanley family. Evidence for this latter visit is based on an entry in the household book of the third Earl of Derby, where it is recorded that on Sunday, September 8th, 1589, "the Company of Lord Essex entertained at night". Among Lord Essex's troop of strolling players was the young William Shakespeare, and it is therefore presumed that he was one of those who entertained the Earl and his guests.

A more certain connection is with the Elizabethan poet, Edmund Spencer, son of a Lancashire cloth worker who went to London to make his fortune. Edmund was educated in London and then went to Cambridge as a "sizar" – a poor scholar who worked as a servant in return for free board and lodging. After he was awarded his M.A. degree in 1576 it is very probable that Spencer went to live with relatives at Hurstwood near Burnley. Here you can still see "Spencer's cottage", and it was in the wooded country around Hurstwood that Spencer is thought to have met and fallen in love with Rosalind to whom he wrote some of his most romantic poems. Spencer's love for Rosalind was unrequited – she married someone else.

CHAPTER II

Jacobean Lancashire

JAMES Stuart, the sixth James to rule over Scotland but the first of that name to be king of England, succeeded Queen Elizabeth in 1603. He was the first of the line of Stuart kings who ruled England for the greater part of the seventeenth century. James had become king of Scotland in 1567 when his mother, Mary, Queen of Scots, abdicated her throne in his favour while she was imprisoned in Lochleven Castle after the battle of Carberry Hill. James had been brought up in an atmosphere of violence, his early years having seen the struggle between Catholics and Presbyterians for power in Scotland. He was the son of Mary's second husband, Lord Darnley, who had been murdered. His mother and the man she later married, James Hepburn, Earl of Bothwell, had been accused of the crime. Violence, murder and lawlessness were rife in the Scotland where James grew up. His mother fled to England where she was kept prisoner for nineteen years, a small reminder of these years remaining at Holker Hall near Cartmel. Mary was never imprisoned there, but in a corner of the beautiful drawing room at Holker is a face panel of the kind which ladies used to protect their complexions from the heat of the fire as they sat close to it to keep warm in the vast cold rooms of Elizabethan mansions. Beautifully embroidered with Chinese symbols, the screen was worked by Mary while she was imprisoned in Derbyshire. Eventually, Mary was executed at Fotheringhay Castle in Northamptonshire in 1587 because she was suspected of being a party to a plot to assassinate Queen Elizabeth. The Roman Catholics who hatched this plot planned to put Mary on the throne of England and restore Roman Catholicism.

It is not surprising when we consider his background and upbringing that James grew up to be a man who went in fear of his life, and that physical violence in any form was abhorrent to him. He always wore thickly padded clothes (which he used till they were in tatters) to protect him from possible attack. James was not an attractive man. This is how Charles Dickens describes him in *A Child's History of England*:

"Our cousin of Scotland was ugly, awkward and shuffling both in mind and person. His tongue was much too large for his mouth, his legs were much too weak for his body, and his dull goggle-eyes stared and rolled like an idiot's. He was cunning, covetous, wasteful, idle, drunken, greedy, dirty, cowardly, a great swearer, and the most conceited man on earth".

But though in some ways James was an object of fun with his padded clothes and rickety legs, he had been well educated and was very learned in many subjects. He has been referred to as "the wisest fool in Christendom" because, although he was wise in book learning, he did not use his wisdom well in dealing with other men or in governing the land. He left a legacy of trouble to his son, Charles I who succeeded him and in whose reign the trouble between king and Parliament reached a climax which resulted in the Civil War.

James was the author of many books described by Charles Dickens as "some of the most wearisome treatises ever read". He wrote at length on the Divine Right of Kings – the theory that kings could do no wrong because they were appointed by God and that no one had any right to interfere with the government of a monarchy. This was the belief which led James into conflict with his Parliaments who were wanting more power.

But it was not always on matters of such political importance that James aired his views. One thing he felt strongly about was tobacco which had been introduced into England during the reign of Queen Elizabeth. Tobacco smoking, which had become popular with many of the gentry, was condemned by James as "a custom lothsome to the eye, hateful to the nose, harmeful to the brain (and) dangerous to the lungs".

Another matter which James made the subject of one of his many books was witchcraft. Today many of us think of witchcraft as superstitious nonsense and associate it with spine-chilling horror films, but in the seventeenth century there was a widespread fear of witches and the evil powers that they had. James I himself was a very superstitious man with a deep-rooted fear of witchcraft. In 1591 a group of so-called witches had been brought to trial in Scotland accused of trying to bring about the death of James by witchcraft. In England as well as in Scotland people believed that there were witches who could work all manner of evil through their lord and master, the devil; and soon after James became king of England a law was passed that death was to be the punishment for "the practice of wicked arts".

In 1597 James wrote his famous book about witchcraft. It was called *Demonology* and it was reprinted in 1603, and widely circulated in England. In the book James describes the terrible and terrifying powers of the witches. They could put curses on their enemies so that they lost use of their limbs, make clay images of them and cause their deaths, harm cattle, raise violent storms and make people love or hate each other. All this they could do because they had sold their souls to the devil who appeared to them usually in the form of an animal, called a familiar, and who had given them the power of life or death over their neighbours. The king's lists of the ways of recognising a witch make fascinating reading and he mentions the tests which should be tried on anyone suspected of being one. The first test was to look for the witch's mark. It was believed that the devil had taken blood from all witches and that somewhere on their bodies there would be the mark which showed where this blood had been drawn. The mark was insensitive to pain; it could be pierced with a needle and the witch would feel nothing at all, nor would blood pour from the wound. If the victim of the test shed tears of pain this was double proof that she was no witch, for a witch could shed only three tears, and these from her left eye only! Another test was "swimming a witch". The unfortunate suspect was bound hand and foot and thrown into the village pond or river. A witch would float on top of the water, for no witch ever drowned; an innocent person would sink and had to be rescued from drowning by the bystanders who always gathered in large numbers to watch the proceedings.

James had a simple explanation of the fact that most suspected of witchcraft were women. "The reason is easie", he writes, "for as that sex is frailer than man is, so it is easier to be entrapped in these grosse snares of the Devil as was over well proved to be true by the Serpent's deceiving of Eve at the beginning".

The circulation of James's book on witchcraft led to witch trials in many parts of the country and among the most famous of all were the trials of the Lancashire witches in 1612 at Lancaster. This brood of witches is often referred to as the Pendle witches because they came from the Forest of Pendle in the shadow of Pendle Hill. Even today there are vast, practically uninhabited areas around Pendle where one can walk for miles and have no company but the wild birds of the lonely moors. In the seventeenth century this county was even wilder – an area crossed by few paths and only a few small hamlets here and there in the wild, bleak moorland country. It was in these small hamlets, cut off from the civilisation of the towns, that strange rumours circulated of the wicked deeds of the witches. Sudden deaths occurred, cattle were smitten with strange diseases, great storms flashed and crashed in the hills – all, the inhabitants thought, due to the dark work of the agents of the devil.

The story of the Lancashire witches has been told in a famous novel by Harrison Ainsworth. His romance is a fascinating account of magic spells, malicious old hags and clay images, all woven round the story of Alison Device and Richard Assheton of Middleton. Parts of the story are based on fact – and the facts we know because the witches were taken for trial to Lancaster and an account of the trials was written by Thomas Potts who was the Clerk of the Court. Potts called his book *A Wonderfulle Discoverie of Witches in the County of Lancaster,* and in it he gives an account of the trials of nineteen men and women brought before the judges at that grim fortress, Lancaster Castle, which since 1176 has been used as a criminal court.

In his book Thomas Potts not only records the trials and confessions of the witches, but also gives us illuminating descriptions of the weird creatures. He tells us that the arch witch of the Lancashire brood, known as Mother Demdike, but whose real name was Elizabeth Southernes, was eighty years old and had been a witch for fifty years. She is referred to by Potts as a "sinke of villainie and mischiefe" and "a damnable and malicious witch". Demdike lived at the Malkin Tower in the forest of Pendle, "a vaste place fit for her profession". Potts says darkly "what shee committed in her time no man knows". She readily confessed when brought before the magistrate, Roger Nowell of Read Hall, that the devil had often appeared to her in the form of a brown dog and that she had cursed Richard Baldwyn, the miller of Wheethead, because he had refused to give her money. Soon after the curse, Baldwyn's daughter had died suddenly and mysteriously. At her trial Demdike gave a detailed account of how she disposed of those she cursed by making clay images of them. "The speediest way to take a man's life away by witchcraft", she said, "is to make a picture of clay like unto the shape of the person whom they mean to kill, and dry it thoroughly. When they would have them be ill, then take a thorn or pin and prick it in that part of the picture you would have any part of the body to consume away, then take that part of the picture and burn it. And when they would have the whole body to consume away, then take the remnant of the saide picture and burn it, and so thereupon by that means the body shall die".

"Next in order to that wicked fire brand of mischiefe,

Lancashire witch country—Downham bridge and Pendle Hill.

Old Demdike", Potts placed Alice Whittle, more usually known by her nickname of Chattox. She is described by Potts as "a very old, withered, spent and decrepit creature, her lips for ever chattering and walking (moving), but no man knew what". Perhaps it was this habit of muttering to herself which had given her the name Chattox. At her trial she accused Demdike of persuading her to become a witch and told how the devil had appeared to her in the form of a spirit called Fancie who had promised that she would do his will. Potts tells us that "in her witchcraft she was always more ready to doe mischiefe to men's goods than to themselves". but she confessed that along with Old Demdike and others she had worked to bring about the death of a certain Robert Nutter by making clay images.

These two, Chattox and Demdike, were the ring leaders of the Pendle Witches. They were the first to be accused along with Alison Device, granddaughter of Demdike, and Anne Redferne, daughter of Chattox. When these four were brought before Roger Nowell and ordered to be taken to

Rough Lee Hall, the home of Alice Nutter who was sentenced to death at the Lancaster witch trials. The building is now divided into four separate dwellings.

Lancaster Assizes, a great meeting of witches was held at Malkin Tower, the home of Old Demdike, on Good Friday 1612. To show their rejection of Christianity the followers of the devil mocked the great Christian festivals, the most sacred fast day of the Christian Church, Good Friday, being celebrated by the witches as their greatest feast day. On this particular Good Friday the Pendle witches, after a great feast of stolen mutton and bacon, made plans to blow up Lancaster Castle with gunpowder, to kill the keeper of the castle, a Mr. Thomas Cowell, and to release all the prisoners. However, news of the meeting at Malkin Tower and the plans of the witches reached the ears of Mr. Roger Nowell at Read Hall, and as a result most of those who had been at the meeting were brought before him, accused of witchcraft, and taken as prisoners over the lonely road through the Trough of Bowland to join Old Demdike and the others at Lancaster Castle. Among these new prisoners was Elizabeth Device, daughter of Demdike. She must have been a hideous creature. The sight of her, "her left eye standing lower than the other, the one looking down and the other looking up", would have been enough to frighten anyone she met even if she had not been known as a witch. In their prison, the Well Tower of Lancaster Castle, the rings and staples by which the poor wretches were chained while waiting for their trial can still be seen.

Old Demdike died in the Well Tower before she could be brought before the judges. The others were nearly all condemned by their own confessions and the evidence given against them by other witches. One who maintained her innocence to the end was Alice Nutter whose home was at Rough Lee. Alice was quite different from the other accused who were poor and had mostly scraped a living by begging from their neighbours (and cursing those who refused to give). She was the wife of a prosperous yeoman farmer. Their home, Rough Lee Hall, is still standing and is now used as four separate dwellings. Perhaps there was jealousy of Alice Nutter who considered herself superior to her neighbours; perhaps she was indeed a notorious witch. Evidence was given by Jennet Device, granddaughter of Old Demdike, that Alice Nutter had been one of the witches at the famous meeting at the Malkin Tower. Alice protested that she was innocent and the judge was determined to give her a fair trial. He arranged what we would nowadays call an identification parade when a suspect is brought before a witness along with innocent people who happen to look rather like him. Each time Jennet identified Alice as the one she had seen at the Malkin Tower and it was mainly on the evidence of this nine-year old girl that Alice Nutter was condemned to death. Potts describes Jennet as "a young infant, raised up through the wonderful work of God" to bring the witches to justice. Other people did not share Pott's regard for Jennet. She seemed to have had no love for any of her family or neighbours and was only too ready to damn them with her evidence. When she was older she was herself brought to trial as a witch in 1633.

Of the nineteen who were tried at Lancaster in August 1612, for "most barbarous and damnable practices, murders, wicked and devilish conspiracies", nine were found not guilty, one (Mother Demdike) died before sentence was passed, and another (Margaret Pearson) was sentenced to stand in the pillory at Clitheroe, Padiham, Whalley and Lancaster and to be imprisoned for one year. The others were all hanged at Lancaster the day after the trials finished.

So ended the most famous of the witch trials in Lancashire. To us witchcraft may seem very weird and part of a world of phantasy, but the memory of the Lancashire witches lingers on in the Pendle district. Tourists still go to Rough Lee to see Alice Nutter's house, and to the churchyard at Newchurch to see the witch's grave. It was in this very churchyard, according to evidence given at the trials that Old Chattox had been observed stealing teeth from dead men's skulls to use in magic charms. Read Hall, where Roger Nowell lived in the early seventeenth century, has since been rebuilt, though his pew in Whalley church still stands as a silent reminder of the magistrate who first found out the witches and brought them to justice. In the same church we can still see the marks on the font where locks held down a cover to prevent the witches from stealing the Holy Water to use in their secret ceremonies. And in spite of the proximity of modern manufacturing towns, there is still a haunting quality in the atmosphere of the "Witch Country", particularly when the mists are down over the Big End of Pendle, that has a compelling atttaction for those in search of background for this strange chapter of Lancashire history.

* * *

Hoghton Tower, a magnificent example of a Tudor manor house built in the late medieval style, stands on the main road between Preston and Darwen. From the road an imposing straight drive leads up to the house built in 1565 by Thomas Hoghton, a friend of the Cardinal Allen of Rossall whom we met in the last chapter. It was up this drive, in 1617, that James I rode with his host Sir Richard de Hoghton at the beginning of a three day visit. But the drive we see now would be unrecognisable to those who gathered there on August 1617 to greet their monarch. A royal visit to Lancashire was such an unusual event that thousands assembled at Hoghton Tower to witness the splendid cavalcade which included the famous Duke of Buckingham, the king's favourite, four earls, five barons, the Bishop of Chester, and a tremendous number of courtiers.

The de Hoghton family had spared no expense in preparing for the arrival of the first Stuart king. Extra wings had been

In the heart of the witch country—the gift shop at Newchurch in Pendle.

built on to the house to provide accommodation for all the retinue of the monarch, and the two largest rooms in the house had been set aside for the king's use and completely re-furnished. A large four-poster bed had been specially made for James by local craftsmen and from the carved canopy hung the most expensive drapings. Tradition has it that the "red carpet" to welcome the royal visitor was of crimson velvet, and as this was laid down the full length of the drive – nearly a mile – you may get some idea of the expense of entertaining "His Royal Sowship". So great was the expense in fact that after the visit the de Hoghton family were in severe financial difficulties and Sir Richard himself spent some of his later years in a debtors' prison. (One family who lived at Bartle Hall, near Preston, heard that the king proposed to visit them and so set fire to their house to avoid having to entertain him. Presumably the cost of rebuilding was less than the expense of acting as hosts to James for a few days). Apart from adding new wings to the house, buying new clothes, new furniture, new tapestries for the walls, pictures, etc., the de Hoghtons had to entertain members of all the important families for miles around because they would want to be presented to the monarch and to join in the festivities.

The people of the area surrounding Hoghton Tower made the royal visit an excuse for a holiday and gathered in thousands to see the king. Stalls had been set up along the drive and entertainers – jugglers, minstrels and acrobats – amused the thronging crowds. Beggars hoped to prevail on the goodwill of the merry-makers, and the sick waited in the hope that the "kings touch", believed to have miraculous healing power, would cure them.

The long-awaited moment came when King James appeared riding with Sir Richard at the head of the gaily dressed cavalcade. James himself was never the man to be extravagant in his dress, but his courtiers were resplendent in their brightly coloured costumes of silk and taffeta then popular with the wealthy. The bobbing plumes of their feathered hats, the shining sleekness of the horses and the gleaming leather boots of the riders all added brightness and glamour to the procession as it progressed through the motley collection of onlookers who would remember and talk about their first sight of King "Jamie" for the rest of their lives.

For three days the king, his retinue and the local gentry hunted in the forested country around Hoghton Tower and had very good sport, though when we study the menus for the king's meals it seems surprising that the party had either time or energy left for hunting. On the first night, after the most important guests had been presented to James, the king was led to the great panelled dining hall. Cooks and scullions had been busy for days preparing the 48 dishes which were "set before the king". Among the items on the menu were "boyld capon, boyld chickens, roste veale, turkie roste, pastie of venison hote, dried hogges cheeke, red deare pye, wild boar pye, pigions, gamon of bacon, quailes, peare tarte and pease buttered". Equally impressive fare was offered throughout the visit including an enormous platter of loin of beef which James seemed to think such an outstandingly magnificent cut of the roast beef of England that he whipped out his sword and dubbed the loin of beef "Sir Loin" – and by this name of sirloin it has been known ever since the ceremony at Hoghton. The table where James knighted the loin of beef is still shown with pride to visitors to the Tower.

Inside the great house Sir Richard and his guests feasted and made merry, entertained by musicians and warmed by great log fires. Outside, the estate tenants and villagers roasted an enormous ox provided for them by Sir Richard, and the noise and merriment went on into the small hours of those August mornings. The people of Lancashire always know how to enjoy themselves and, seeing their king in festive mood, they presented a petition to him during this visit to Hoghton asking that amusements and entertainments which had been forbidden on Sundays in the reign of Elizabeth could be indulged in again. They were delighted when James gave his consent that, after they had attended service at church, the people of England could make merry dancing round the maypole, morris dancing or on hobby horses, but he would not allow them to play football – in those days a much rowdier and rougher game than it is when played under present-day rules. (In the Middle Ages and Tudor times football, often played with a pig's bladder for a ball, had any number of players, and usually the winning side was the one with the least number of broken arms or legs!).

This petition from the people of Lancashire was the prelude to the *Book of Sports* which James published in 1618, and which did away with the old Puritanical idea that the people should not be allowed any pleasure at all on Sundays. James declared that the good people of England should not be deprived of or discouraged from any lawful recreations such as dancing, archery, leaping, vaulting, or from having May games, Whitsun ales or morris dancing, nor from setting up maypoles and other sports "providing that the same be had in due and convenient time, without impediment or neglect of divine service". Once again it became lawful for churches to be decorated and for such ancient ceremonies as rush bearing to take place, but "unlawful games" such as bear- and bull-baiting were still forbidden, as was the playing of bowls by the common people! For most of the people of England this was one of the most popular of the edicts of the first King James, and it may well be that it was the sight of the people of Lancashire enjoying the holiday to celebrate his visit to Hoghton Tower which made James relax the laws against Sunday recreations.

* * *

The front cover drawing of King James I knighting the "Sir Loin" of beef at Hoghton Tower is by E. Jeffrey. The back cover drawing is a contempory print of Elizabethan sport—a wolf hunt. All uncredited photographs are by the author.

The photograph on page 12 is by Elsam, Mann and Cooper, and is published by permission of Liverpool Corporation.